EMPATH

A Guide To Understanding, Defending &
Nurturing Your Precious Gift

By Luna Sidana

Table of Contents

Introduction

It takes all kinds to make the world. All souls on this planet have different strengths and weaknesses, distinct personality traits and temperaments, as well as different ways of seeing the world and living their lives. A curious quality unique to the human experience is the great capacity for empathy.

"Empathy" is defined as the ability to understand or identify with another individual's emotions and experiences. It differs from sympathy, which is an external sort of caring (and sometimes pity) for the pain and misfortunes of others.

Rather, empathy is the mental act of "walking in someone else's shoes", and having the sensitivity to experience a situation outside of oneself as if it were one's own.

Consider an evenly distributed bell curve graph:

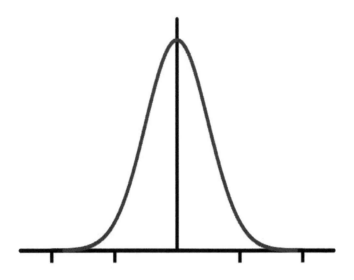

Most of the world's populace has normal, or moderate, levels of empathy. They are neither callous nor are they overly compassionate, and could be called "decent human beings". As we move out from the center of average levels of empathy, we find fewer people on either end of the spectrum who are capable of feeling either less or more empathy.

The extremes of the chart represent a minority of

the population who either are almost completely lacking in empathy, or have an unusually heightened facility for it. The latter group is the focus of this book, and are known as "empaths". As you are reading this book right now, this is most likely where you belong as well.

Empaths are highly sensitive people with the natural ability to feel and tap into others' affective and cognitive states. Most empaths are born this way, though the skills can be cultivated with practice and may develop over the course of a lifetime. It means being able to deeply feel someone else's experience to the point where separating one's energy from someone else's may be very difficult.

This sensitivity is not restricted to an awareness of other humans. Sensing subtle details about animals, plants, and universal rhythms is also possible, and many empaths are attuned to a combination of these areas.

The awareness goes beyond logical conclusions based on concrete and observable information; empaths possess a deep sense of knowing that often defies reasoning.

Another important distinction is that empaths,

unlike other intuitive people, have a strong tendency to be compassionate and a have the desire to alleviate others' suffering.

Recognizing oneself as an empath is not as easy or obvious as it would appear. These traits are typically present their whole lives but only accurately identified later on, if ever.

The experiences of empaths are often confusing, and they may chalk it up to something that cannot be understood, or settle for an unsatisfying explanation.

Empaths are individuals, and will differ from person to person depending on their varying degrees of empathy, area of sensitivity, level of insight, cultural background, gender, and willingness to accept their gifts. Identifying others as empaths can be equally challenging, considering how their sensitivities manifest and are handled.

The following is a checklist you can use to identify yourself or someone else as an empath (the more points that are checked, the likelier it is that the person in question has the gift of strongly developed empathy):

- An unusually strong sense of intuition. Empaths are sensitive creatures and frequently shy, quiet, introspective, and observant. Intelligence is above average.

- Being extremely sensitive to and aware of others feelings. You usually try to comfort and help those in pain. Can also extend to animals and other living things. This behavior usually begins in childhood.

- Feeling other peoples' emotions as if they were happening first hand. Often developing the symptoms of people in your environment (physical and emotional).

- Feeling things in life much more keenly that others, both pain and pleasure. This includes having a rich inner experience, an active imagination, and being deeply touched by beauty. A sensitivity to spirituality is very common.

- Being kinder, more caring, compassionate, giving, insightful, and helpful than most. You are easily upset by suffering and cruelty in the world. You may have a hard time coping with and understanding unkind behavior from others.

- Being easily overwhelmed and drained by crowds, or negative situations and people.

- Frequently needing some "alone time" to prevent overload. You may prefer to keep own life organized in an attempt not to get overwhelmed.

- Lower back, digestive, and other stress related problems. Fatigue and low stamina are very common. Emotional problems and more severe health conditions are also possible.

- Wondering if you are crazy or imagining things.

- Having the sense of being hit by "waves" of information from time to time.

- A low pain threshold, sensory

sensitivities, and/or being extremely sensitive to medications and various stimulants like caffeine and alcohol.

- Feeling responsible for other people's actions, feelings, and thoughts, or inappropriate guilt in reaction to others' decisions.

- Feeling misunderstood or misinterpreted. May have been described as overly emotional, reading too much into things, or just being too sensitive.

- Being a wonderful listener. People often feel better just by talking to you.

- Having the tendency to attract needy and manipulative people who take advantage of you, or those going through a hard time.

This book is a practical guide intended to help empaths, someone who loves one, or anyone who's simply curious about the subject and wants to learn more.

The theory behind magnified empathy, and society's views on the feminine trait of intuition vs. the masculine strength of logic will begin the dialogue.

A description of life as an empath as well as its pros and cons follows, and then information about those who are particularly hazardous to such a sensitive person.

Pragmatic tips will be given to protect oneself from draining people, prevent future difficulties, and maintain overall balance. Lastly, suggestions for developing one's gifts and using them in a positive way will be addressed.

Chapter 1:

Oneness

People who are different from the masses often feel out of place. It can be even more problematic when the dissimilarity is subtle and seemingly intangible.

Empaths know they are unlike the majority, and are relieved on the infrequent occasions when they meet people more like themselves. Still, the question remains: What makes you, as an empath, unique? And why are you the way you are?

The universe is an ocean of energy. A plethora of ancient mystics have long taught this, and modern science is finally starting to catch up. Physicists describe all things as being composed of energy, and support the notion that we are all connected.

More than that, all things are made from the same material — and this mass is never created, nor is it destroyed. It simply is and shifts form.

Particles viewed under powerful microscopes reveal atoms as much less solid than previously thought. Instead, scientists see vibrating, energetic fields composed of light and sound. Life suddenly acquires a much more mysterious, magical quality when considering these findings.

Furthermore, living and nonliving things have an electromagnetic field of energy that extends beyond the physical barriers of their structures.

These fields, or auras, have been described in details by the ancients, not to mention a whole host of other details about the nature of the universe and how energy works.

Fields are everywhere, and they radiate from people, animal, plants and minerals. They overlap and interact on a constant basis. The Earth itself has a field.

So, imagine life in an ordinary way. Human beings and other forms of life interact with one another and share space constantly. If someone is tapped on the shoulder or called by name, the body and senses register the stimuli and there is a response. Falling into a prickly bush engages pain sensors as input from this unpleasant interaction occurs.

It all comes down to relationships, and the exchange of energy among different variables. Few would argue with this simple explanation because it is observable, and something that people experience on a daily basis. But the human saga is more far nuanced than this, and the world is experienced on much deeper levels.

Feelings and thoughts are not visible to the average person, yet most would also recognize these are "real". It is widely accepted that it is possible to feel when someone else is very angry, sad, anxious, or happy, and most will have those stories of how there was a time when the energy in the room shifted the instant someone feeling something strongly walked in.

There are also occasions when people say they just knew what someone else was thinking, as if they could read their mind. This type of information exists, but is much vaguer and harder to nail down than things that happen in the physical world.

Some people are much more intuitive than others, and those close to them will know that these people pick up on information that escapes nearly everyone else.

Organisms function through a transfer of energy in which nourishment enters the system and waste products are eliminated. They are subject to fluctuating environmental conditions, and do their best to function well under ever changing circumstances. People eat, drink, and breathe, and have the necessary bodily functions to discard what the system does not need.

The same process occurs on a subtler level; humans absorb energy from their environments as well. An energy vibrating at an unseen frequency. This energy can be blocked or taken in, depending on what the organism allows, and the strength of the system. In general, the more open a person is, the more they can absorb.

As an empath, you have the uncanny ability to tap into subtle information poorly available to most. Feelings and thoughts are so real that their impact is similar to the corresponding action.

A tender thought will feel like a caress, whereas a feeling of anger mimics the sensation of being slapped. The world is a maze of information, seen and unseen. It is very, very typical for empaths to be like great sponges, soaking up everything in their vicinity.

Being flooded with input happens regularly if you have not yet learned how to manage your abilities. Your awareness of vibrations occurring on an invisible plane can be similar to what you experience on a physical level, and the impact on your wellbeing is equally significant.

The talent also transcends normal boundaries of time and space. The fact that auras radiate beyond physical boundaries means that empaths can receive information about someone or something's current state before they are close enough to know based on their five senses. As such, another person's emotions may be accurately perceived without access to cues like body language and tone of voice.

Some empaths are able to read a person's auric field, and know things about them from the past or in the future. It is also possible for some to be aware of events happening at a distance, with no direct contact to the situation at all. They just know.

Very simply, an empath lives with the knowledge that barriers among beings are superficial. We are all one mass of energy sharing the same space. It doesn't matter if we are in different bodies, different countries, or different times. The energy remains the same, and the ability to access it lies inside every person.

The wisest people of many different cultures have always known this, and were aware of these and other extraordinary psychic powers. Indians used the term "Siddhi" to describe these abilities, and said they are latent in all humans because the universe lies within. The intelligence of the universe is all-knowing, all-present, all-powerful, and timeless. Humans, according to this philosophy, are simply a microcosm of the whole.

There are many incredible stories of mystics from around the world knowing things they should not be able to, displaying superhuman feats, and accurately predicting world events. Some spiritual teachers will pick up on their students' thoughts and use this as a tool.

Most people, however, operate in ignorance of the light that shines within every soul, and function at a severely limited level compared to what is possible.

Siddhis arise naturally through the process of spiritual growth, as the awareness of the true nature of the universe and the self is gradually understood. An empath feeling another person's trials and tribulations as if they were first hand experiences is knowing that, "The other person is me".

Reincarnation theory helps shed more light on why empaths have an evolved degree of awareness. It is said that souls are all fundamentally the same, and are animated by the same spirit. Life on earth starts in a primitive way at the level of minerals. After many cycles, the being gradually becomes more and more complex and finally graduates to the level of the plant, the animal, and — eventually — the human.

A human birth is the most precious gift of all, because people are the only beings with insight. Being born at this level is hard won, and those who recognize its value will not waste it or remain ignorant of its preciousness.

Most other organisms on Earth operate primarily from instinct, and lacks the developmental complexity to make decisions on a spiritual level. Humans are the only creatures in the natural world who can become aware of their inner divinity. Once a soul reaches the level of the human, decisions must be made.

Every time a person chooses to be kind, compassionate and good, the development proceeds in that direction. These decisions move one closer to the understanding of the all-pervasive love of creation.

The same happens when people go against their

conscience and make poor decisions. But being highly sensitive and intuitive does not automatically equate to being a loving soul. Some intuitives are selfishly motivated, and others deliberately develop their abilities with the purpose to exploit. Still others begin with good intentions, only to lose their way and become drunk with their power.

Closely observing small children reveals their already present personality traits and tendencies, and empaths are usually loving souls early on. They begin their life at a higher level of sensitivity, and display a higher level of attunement to the laws of the universe. Many also have a previous history of spiritual work and devotion.

Chapter 2:

The Feminine/Masculine Polarity & Empathy

It is said that if the universe was visible to its inhabitants in the way in which it was created, the only thing visible would be light. The light would be dazzling, pure, and beautiful. The light would convey the love and tenderness that sparked the manifestation of the world. This is the internal state of all beings, and lives in every one at all times.

However, because almost all of humanity is operating with distorted perceptions, life is filtered through this lens and produces shadows. These shadows are called duality — or seeing life in pairs of opposites. Every light casts a shadow, and everything has a complement. There is hot and cold, active and passive, high and low. Even joy is not immune from sorrow for balance.

For every action, there is a reaction, and the two opposites fit together and are neutral and whole when combined.

China's philosophical school of Taoism describes duality with the terms Yin and Yang, and teaches that freedom is attained when we break beyond these polarities.

This Yin and Yang of life governs anything out of synch with the true oneness of the universe, and means that life is subject to ups and down. In the meantime, one can learn to live harmoniously by aligning oneself with life's natural rhythms and learning to flow effortlessly.

It is all about finding a fine balance, where one is non-reactive and handles situations gracefully as they arise. In China, this is referred to as "Wu-Wei", and means "not forcing". It describes the easy, fluid way of which things in life open in their own time, according to their specific nature.

The individual's job, then, is harmonizing one's energy with that of the universe. Empaths, by nature, are more aware of different kinds of subtle, energetic cycles, and have a predisposition towards working well with them.

A major categorization of the Yin and Yang energies is distinguished in terms of gender. Yang energy, the masculine element (meaning "sunny side"), is active, hot, light, positively charged, and connected to day and the sun. "Shady side" Yin energy is feminine, passive, cool, dark, negatively charged, and related to nighttime and lunar energy.

While Yin and Yang qualities are not exactly the

same as male and female, the attributed traits tend to describe the corresponding gender.

Simultaneously, both sexes are a mix of both Yang and Yin, and individuals are on a spectrum when it comes to gender related tendencies. Some women are very masculine, and some men have strong feminine qualities.

Other women are extremely feminine, and some men very masculine. Yet, like the aforementioned bell curve, the majority of people fall within a range of typical male and female behaviors particular to their gender.

Most people will have certain qualities and skills associated with their biology. It is common knowledge that men and women frequently talk about how puzzled they are by the opposite sex. It has been a basis for both humor and frustration for ages, and is more recently being explained in terms of hormones and other physiological mechanisms.

Still others have a balanced, sometimes androgynous quality, and it is not uncommon for empaths to exist somewhere in this middle ground. Being unusually attuned to the other gender is another sign of the ability to go beyond the parameters of the small self, and identify with other ways of experiencing life. It is also an indication of knowing what it is like to be a different kind of person in past lives.

People may reincarnate in human form many, many times in various ethnicities, religions, cultures, sexual preferences, level of physical functioning, socioeconomic statuses and gender. Each incarnation into a special kind of existence serves as a lesson in seeing a different facet of the world, and appreciating life in a fresh way from a new angle.

Openness and understanding of people who vary from oneself speaks to an unconscious wisdom; that the other person's current lifestyle could very well have been one's own.

Most civilizations of old usually represented both the female and male aspects of divinity in their spirituality, whether or not the culture itself was patriarchal. There were both gods and goddesses who enjoyed equal stature in the heavens, and represented two sides of the same coin of the human experience.

The Creator was both mother and father, and transcended the confines of gender. It can be seen in places like ancient Egypt, Greece, and Mesoamerica, and this tradition is still alive today in paths like Hinduism.

However, the Goddess has all but disappeared in the highly prevalent Abrahamic religions of Christianity, Judaism, and Islam. She is preserved in figures like the Virgin Mary, but God is most definitely a man in these traditions, where masculine qualities reign supreme and are considered ideal.

Independence, boldness, and rational logic are praised and considered far superior to the qualities of interdependence, sensitivity, and intuition normally ascribed to the female sex.

In most cultures, men already enjoy a higher status, and the western world has become a decisive and influential player on the planet over the past few centuries. Western values are affecting Eastern and tribal cultures around the world as well, and the preference for stereotypically male attributes has grown

Nevertheless, perhaps ironically, women tend to have a higher quality of living and enjoy greater gender parity in the Western world).

There has been a definite devaluing of the Goddess and what she represents. Masculine qualities are just as valuable as feminine ones, but they lose their power when their counterpart is diminished. Yang needs Yin and cannot stand alone, and vice versa.

Being a whole person means operating from both places. In many ways, being a female empath is easier, because they are embracing a traditionally female ability. However, women's intuitions are often dismissed (especially by men), and trusting oneself can be hard for many females.

While a woman's authority and power are regularly minimized (a social behavior both men and other women are guilty of), male empaths face different challenges, in which being sensitive is seen as a threat to their masculinity. Many men are socialized not to feel, and being overly perceptive is often said to indicate weakness.

Being accepted and understood by other males can be tough, and male empaths may hide their gifts for fear of ridicule and rejection. Additionally, though many women say they want thoughtful men, they do not always appreciate a male who is too sensitive.

It may be worth to mention that some Indian traditions theorize gender in an opposite fashion compared their fellow Oriental counterparts. Female energy, "Shakti", is the active energy of the universe responsible for creation. It is the desire for one to become many, and manifests forms in the universe out of the primordial void. Male "Shiva" energy is passive, witnesses what Shakti creates, and takes no active part in the birth of the universe.

Shakti represents awareness with choice, and Shiva is choiceless, passive consciousness. When taking a breath, the action of breathing belongs to Shakti while the pause afterwards is governed by Shiva. Most of our lives is all about Shakti. It is not until we quiet the mind that we become aware of Shiva. Shakti is terrestrial and of the earth while Shiva is of the heavens. In some parts of India, the sun is feminine and the moon is considered masculine.

Scholar, author, and teacher Joseph Campbell described how Shiva and Shakti apply to human relationships. He says the female "activates" the male, which then makes him take action. Then, she has to live with the results. He also claims the female provides the energy that drives the relationship. The man, he says, is just along for the ride.

The Hindu female deities run the gamut of being gentle, tender, and nurturing, to ferocious, warlike, and sometimes outright frightening. This spectrum of femininity is shared by other traditions as well. Shiva and Shakti are the equivalents of Yin and Yang, and — like Taoism — they are interdependent and two halves of the same whole.

The goal of breaking beyond duality involves transcending Shiva-Shakti awareness the same way Taoists seek to move beyond Yin and Yang. And though Shiva and Shakti are in fact one, unified entity, there are groups whom devalue Shakti because Shiva is perceived as superior and closer to the goal. But like Yin and Yang, Shiva is nothing without Shakti.

At the end of the day, it is always best to fully accept every aspect of yourself. Doing this is saying "Yes!" to life, and opening up to a wide range of possibilities. As an empath, you will be happiest when you embrace who you are, and are willing to explore what life may hold. As we will discuss, your skills can be extremely valuable, both to yourself and to others.

Chapter 3:

The Ups & Downs of Being An Empath

Being an empath is definitely not easy. It is human nature to fear insight and new information. Anything new threatens one's current identity and means opening up more and more. The greatest threat to the ego is its demise in which humans no longer need a separate identity, and are instead absorbed into the sea of oneness.

Empaths get a small taste of this every day, as they are conscious of the many impulses in the world beyond their own. Imagine all of the things people are thinking, feeling, and experiencing. Most of it is kept under the surface in normal living.

Now imagine what it would be like if all of that information spilled out into the environment. It would be like being pummeled by ocean waves or trying to escape a minefield.

The stimuli can be painful, confusing, or simply distracting and unnecessary, and doing very simple daily activities can be a struggle.

Many cultures teach that the world is a place of suffering and pain, and the empath's experience of anguish in the universe certainly supports this. Furthermore, empaths can't always distinguish the source of their feelings and can be easily affected by outside situations. Some empaths become reclusive because they are so overwhelmed. Something as simple as grocery shopping can become an arduous task requiring great fortitude. Even the empaths who are able to manage on a day to day basis will undoubtedly have issues in other areas.

Relationships are a huge part of most people's lives, and impact just about every aspect. Empaths are so attuned to other peoples' emotions and experiences that it can be hard to know how to appropriately handle situations. Sometimes they simply have too much information that muddles and overcomplicates things.

Having access to others' secrets can leave people feeling naked or uneasy. Being the only one in the room who sees the true underlying dynamics of a situation can be isolative and lonely.

Unhealthy relationships are especially tough, because it is hard to know where one person ends and the other begins. At these times, it is a challenge to act in the best interests of oneself and the relationship, because the empath is acutely aware of both sets of needs. Unfortunately, the awareness of the other person's needs often overwhelms and outweighs those of the sensitives'.

Empaths have a nasty habit of trying to solve conflict at the expense of themselves, and will often make changes to appease the other party. They may have been responding to subtle needs automatically for years, and were not aware of it. Sensitives often go out of their way to balance a situation when doing so is usually not their responsibility.

Feeling another person's stress can be so painful that is easier to try to make them feel better than stand their ground and go against the other person's wishes. Besides, there is often an element of confusion in regards to what is right for the empath, and empaths often suffer from disproportionate guilt and a fear or being "selfish".

Codependency is something many sensitives need to work on. If unaddressed, boundaries become increasingly fuzzier and the relationship becomes increasingly diseased. The empath is not helping, only enabling the dysfunction and denying themselves of health.

Healthier relationships can be a challenge as

well. People who are loving and well-intentioned simply may not understand, or misinterpret an empath's experiences. Empaths may be chalked up to being too emotional and told to shake it off. Sensitivities may be dismissed (not necessarily unkindly) and alternate explanations provided.

Loved ones may expect things from empaths that is hard for them to give, and be impatient of the sensitive soul when crowds are avoided, or being in a bad neighborhood is almost intolerable. Some may be sympathetic to empaths, but feel helpless as they watch their friend or family member struggle. Empaths usually become frustrated at how hard it is to explain what they feel, and how hard it is to make other people get it.

Empaths may hide or minimize their experiences in fear of being judged and rejected, or fear being a burden to others. Others will simply give up trying to make other people understand, and will stick to a few people whom they feel comfortable around.

Something very important that you need to be aware of is how your sensitivity may affect your health. Because empaths absorb energy and are often healers, they tend to sop up large amounts of negative energy. They generally take in the negativity faster than it can be discharged, and the result is disharmony and disease. Depression, anxiety, and mood swings are typical empath problems that stem from retaining too many issues in their environment.

Emotional issues can also be rooted in the complex and painful way they go through life. Other symptoms are more physical in nature, and manifest as conditions like chronic pain, chronic fatigue, and fibromyalgia. Unfortunately, it is not unheard of for empaths to turn to self-destructive behaviors like alcoholism, drug abuse, or overeating as a way to numb themselves from the constant stimulation.

Some sensitives become overly intellectual and cut off from their emotions. They learn how to block everything as a way to survive, including their empathic abilities. Work, home, school, hobbies, etc. are all affected, and functioning in one or more of these areas is typical. A seemingly unrelated issue like financial stress could be a direct correlation to the empath's difficulty focusing and performing on the job.

While reading through this you might think that living as an empath is a huge challenge, and it sure can be. However, it isn't all bad! The empath's life is, if nothing else, highly interesting. And it is misleading to portray all of these gifted individuals as miserable souls who never quite get the hang of coping with life, or as people who won't trust themselves or develop their potential. This is true of some, but there are always those who cultivate their talents and live a fulfilling life.

Sensitive people often have parents or other family members with similar proclivities, and these adults may recognize the behavior for what it is early on. Fortunate empaths will have adults who help them understand and cope with their sensitivity. Even ones who do not have this head start may later in life find peers who are either empaths as well or encouraging to them.

Still others will simply figure it out as they go and adapt well, whether or not they have the words to describe what is happening. And there are always the tenacious who refuse to listen to what other people say and eventually blossom through determination.

An empath may manifest as a socially awkward person who avoids crowds, but it could also be a vivacious creature with a lust for life, or a quiet, content, introspective soul.

The word "struggle" has a negative connotation, but it is foolish to assume that struggling is fundamentally unhealthy. In life, stress can be either negative or positive. Negative stress is not constructive, and damages the wellbeing of an individual. Living in a polluted city where cancer rates are far above the national average is stressing the system, and causing disease that could easily be prevented.

Positive stress can be likened to the massive amounts of pressure carbon endures to become a diamond. When people are sore and grumbling after exercising muscles they did not know they had, their pain is a sign of extra strain placed on the system. But this stress is clearly advantageous, and part of a larger plan to increase vigor and strength.

Many serious spiritual practitioners undergo severe ordeals of physical and emotional discomfort to test their stamina. Fasting, sleep deprivation, and exposure to the elements are not unheard of ways to transcend one's perceived limits, and discover a wealth of previously unimaginable power within. Likewise, the stress associated with being an empath is not necessarily negative.

Life is full of lessons, and the most valuable ones

are often painful. The trials may unlock something deep inside that otherwise would have lain dormant. What appears to be negative stress can be transformed into positive stress, but discretion must be used to prevent unnecessary suffering.

Living life as an empath could be described as both a blessing and a curse. Feeling life on a deeper level gives a greater appreciation of existence, but the confusion and awareness of the world's pain is definitely thorny. Yet, this description is shallow at best, and does not speak to the treasures awaiting the empath who learns to gain control over their facilities.

Life is a strange, surprising thing and, just when it seems that nothing new can be found, there is yet another discovery.

Being an empath means that you are instinctually attuned to the deeper layers of life, and that you have greater access to experiencing them. Committing to the exploration of such baffling territory can be frightening and overwhelming at first, and you may find yourself longing to be "normal".

Being gifted involves making certain sacrifices,

and sacrificing the comfort of belonging to the mainstream will be worth it for the much more satisfying rewards ahead.

Empaths are often natural healers, and can be adept physicians, nurses, midwives, chiropractors, massage therapists, and energy healers. For those with sensitivities to plants and animals, gardening or animal training may be second nature. The arts may be the perfect avenue to express the empath's experience of the universe. Their access to wisdom gives them insight that can be of use to others, and being a sensitive soul can make one a superb partner, child, parent, coworker, supervisor or friend.

Being an empath means developing an unusual degree of closeness in healthy relationships. The intimacy, be it physical, emotional, or spiritual, is much more intense, and there is a degree of fulfillment that comes from such a close union that can be difficult to describe. These relationships are not always with other people. They can also be with nature, animals, plants, stones, or the universe at large.

Others will answer the call to spiritual studies and find their niche. Not all will feel the need to be open about their abilities, and instead lead quiet, fulfilling lives full of richness. People who live and speak the truth of the universe are far more beneficial to society than all of the wealthy philanthropists put together.

Empaths are especially attuned to the beauty of creation, and their recognition automatically affects the world by raising the collective vibration of humanity to a higher level. So, as an empath you are full of potential — now the task at hand is learning to accept your gift, and transform it into a positive, purposeful way of being.

Chapter 4:

Living Day-to-Day As An Empath

Zen Buddhism has a wonderful tradition of storytelling. There is a lovely vignette that tells the tale of two poor street performers, an old man and a little girl. Their act involves the child balancing on the elder's shoulders. Doing well is vital, because their livelihood depends on good tips.

The old man anxiously tells the little girl that they should look out for each other, by concentrating on keeping their partner balanced. The little girl is wiser, and disagrees. She says that if she focuses on her balance and he focuses on his, both will remain poised and their act will be a success.

Each individual has a path in life, and everyone has a wise, all knowing inner voice that effectively navigates the person when heeded. Listening to, trusting, and following this guidance system can be difficult. Many of us struggle with self-confidence, and doubt our intuition so often. What makes it even more complicated is how other people's desires contradict the voice's instructions.

Most people know how hard it is to follow their instincts when others are skeptical, critical, or anxious about their decisions. It is said that when one embraces the inner expert, balance is found, and life shifts dramatically. Doors swing open in miraculous ways, and life flows smoothly instead of being a series of struggles. The problem is that nearly everyone pays more attention to others than they do to themselves.

Most are so busy thinking about what others are doing (and frequently wishing they were doing something else) that few people know how to focus on themselves. Empaths are aware of so many souls that it is easy to lose their own voice amidst the cacophony. A task that already requires conviction and focus is much more complex and difficult.

As an empath, you may not always be understood or appreciated by others — or even yourself — and believing that these strange experiences are not an indication of weakness or mental instability can be hard to swallow. Deciding that they are a blessing may seem ridiculous and even funny at first.

Yet, that inner voice is never truly absent, and chances are that you have always had a vague awareness that your "problems" fit into a bigger picture, and indicate something special and unusual.

Whether or not other people endorse this belief is immaterial. Thriving requires quite a lot of ignoring, and it is in your (not to mention everyone on the planet's) best interest to take a leap of faith, and follow that strange, baffling guru that lies within.

History has endless accounts of how talented, innovative people struggled for years with doubt and low-self-esteem, and had to resist the incredulous way others viewed their efforts. Famous inventors, for example, were often told they were wasting their time and would never succeed. Visionaries are able to perceive and imagine concepts that elude the masses. Empaths share the capacity for seeing beyond the norm, and their talents can lead to great things when properly developed and nurtured.

The most important lesson you need to master is that of healthy boundaries. Being able to distinguish your energy from another's, and keeping them separate, will change your life in dramatic, unforeseen ways.

Bewildering situations will become clear, and thus make life simpler and easier to go through. Acting in your own best interest ceases to be so difficult, and the fear of hurting other people and being selfish is put into perspective. Everything else falls into place naturally once boundaries are firm.

The difference between living in harmony with your gift and feeling overwhelmed and bombarded comes down to one simple word: Balance. Proper boundaries are crucial to equilibrium, and attaining subsequent higher levels of development.

Consider this: For a cell to function well, it must be both permeable and firm. It must be flexible enough so sustenance can enter and waste can exit, but it cannot be too flexible, either; The cell would collapse without a steady structure to support its existence. Humans are the same way, and finding that balance can be delicate for many.

Empaths, by nature, are usually very permeable, and tend to lack the proper level of firmness to tolerate the information exchange. Sensitivity then becomes hypersensitivity, and this creates pain. Poor boundaries are the norm for empaths and/or having overly rigid ones in an attempt to protect. Creating a healthy boundary is about becoming attuned to one's own needs, which makes it easy to have healthy, reciprocal relationships.

Weak boundaries are a detriment to both parties, not just the you. An enmeshed relationship keeps everyone weak, and a codependent one only enables the needy and keeps the enabler stuck. Being in a relationship with a bully is another vicious, self-perpetuating cycle. Even a relationship with a healthy person will flounder and ultimately fail from a lack of clarity.

Taking responsibility for the feelings of others, being "too nice", and giving too much are common pitfalls for a highly sensitive person. The first issue speaks to an understanding that we are all one, and another person's experience is mine as well; however, in doing so, the empath is disregarding the fact that each person is responsible for his or her own decisions while in physical form. Worse, it is indulging in pity, not compassion.

Knowing the difference between the two is powerful and life changing. Pity is feeling sorry for someone. There is nothing constructive about pity. It is like saying, "Oh, that poor person. What happened is so sad. I feel so bad for them and wish things had been different". The person who thinks this way chooses to suffer with the object of the pity.

The funny thing is, pity strips people of both

their power and responsibility. Instead of understanding that the person is experiencing consequences of events and decisions, the person becomes a victim. It is — in all actuality — quite patronizing, and fails to see that everything in life is an opportunity for growth.

Compassion is much different, which is lovingly recognizing another person's suffering without a trace of pity. It is also understanding that the person is not helpless, and does not need to be saved. Pity leads to enabling; compassion fuels genuine assistance.

Being overly polite or "too nice" happens out of fear of hurting other people's feelings, and a lack of courage to say what one really thinks. Most people are invested in their current mindset and just want other people to agree with them. Often, the empath is unconsciously tuned into the other person's frequency and ends up giving them what they want.

Giving too much falls into a similar category of meeting the mind's broadcasted needs. It is also characteristic of low self-esteem, in which one feels the need to prove one's worth. This behavior drops sharply once someone feels good about themselves.

All of these behaviors were chosen by the empath, and the underlying reason why may not be cheerfully acknowledged. The truth is that it is easier and safer to invest one's time and energy into other people's issues, than developing one's own potential. At the end of the day, it is your responsibility to draw the line in the sand about what will and will not be tolerated.

The voice is one of a human's most powerful tools. Saying "no" is one of the most impactful things you can do as an empath. It is so simple, yet immensely effective, and automatically reinforces the boundaries of your aura. By doing so, you are making a clear statement about what will and what will not be allowed into your life. The universe listens, and will continue to send unwanted things into your life if you keep letting it without speaking up.

Many people have a hard time saying "no", and think the consequences of doing so will be more than they can handle. This is rarely the case. Even the smallest incidents are indications of deeper problems with the voice. You may feel guilty initially when refusing others, but eventually this fades, and will be replaced with feelings of strength and empowerment.

The throat chakra governs not only the ability to

communicate with others, but also the ability to hear one's inner voice, and listen to the murmurs of the cosmos. When this energetic center is clear, it is easy to speak up for your needs without violating other people's rights.

Equally as important, if not more, it means trusting the divine guidance inside. The throat's functions extend to creativity as well. This is the sort of creativity that goes beyond self-expression on a personal level, and conveys a far-reaching intelligence sensed internally.

Using one's voice helps open this chakra, and so does being silent. The quiet makes it easier to hear this voice. A problem that plagues many is not that one is out of touch with the throat, but that one refuses to use it or follow its instructions.

The human body contains multiple energetic centers in addition to the throat, and the most fundamental of these is the root chakra. Our first center, located at the base of the spine, is what tethers us to the earth. Having a solid connection to the earth plane is what makes one steady.

It is also essential for those who desire to develop more advanced levels of awareness. The natural sensitivity possessed by an empath is a sign that upper chakras are already more developed than the average person.

However, opened upper energy centers with weak lower ones causes a strong inflow without proper support. These kinds of people consequently have trouble functioning in the material world, and struggle with basic needs. Staying grounded is absolutely essential to functioning in this world, and developing this area is a priority if the aforementioned description applies to you.

Signs of not being rooted include feeling spacey, anxiety, having a floating sensation, confusion, dissociation from the body, lack of stamina and stability, and depression. Having firm contact with the ground is like being a house with a strong foundation. It keeps the house steady even in changing environmental conditions. Discomfort from awareness of the waves of psychic information will diminish, or even disappear, when the root chakra is properly engaged.

Some of the easiest ways to ground yourself involve small, simple movements that can even be done in public when feeling disconnected from the body:

- Looking down by tilting your chin towards your chest engages the root and will instantly stabilize the system.

- Another way is by creating sensations in your feet. Wiggling your toes will send energy downwards and, if possible, massaging your feet helps tremendously. The inner portion of the heel on the sole of the foot is the reflexology point for the base chakra, and is an especially potent hotspot.

- Splashing cold water on your face, repeating your name, age and date of birth to yourself, and becoming aware of any sensations like the presence of clothing against skin all reconnect you to the earth plane and the physical body.

You can also try the following meditation to help ground yourself. It is particularly good when done on chaotic days. Being proactive and performing this prior to a hectic situation is best:

1. Find a quiet space. Sitting on the floor is especially helpful. A kneeling position with legs hip-width apart and glutes resting on the heels is even better. (If the

glutes do not reach the heels easily, a folded blanket can be placed in between to cushion the gap.)

2. Keep your back straight and take a moment for the mind to quiet.

3. Feel in contact with the earth and say, "I surrender to the support of the earth."

4. Imagine tree roots growing down from the tailbone deep into the ground and absorbing vibrant, life sustaining energy from the earth into the body.

5. Feel anchored, safe and secure. Maintain this imagery until calm has been established.

Ancient teachings declare that the earth is not mankind's real home. It is merely a stop along the road on the journey back to a divine state of being. Several of the world's cultures use an upside-down tree — the "Tree of Life" — to represent humanity's actual condition.

The tree, with its roots in the air, illustrates how

our true roots are not in the ground, but in the heavens. People are spiritual beings having a physical experience, not the other way around. As an empath, you are naturally more attuned to this insight, and may have trouble feeling comfortable in your current abode.

Sometimes there is a degree of discord and even rejection of the physical world. This leads to a multitude of problems and creates existential angst. Therefore, some empaths may be reluctant to reconnect to the earth element, or underestimate its importance in the subconscious desire to go back home. These tendencies will only generate more suffering. Accepting your current form changes everything for the better.

Chapter 5:

"Energy Vampires"

There are three major types of symbiotic interactions. In the first, one party benefits and the other is neutral. In the second, both parties benefit. And, in the third, one party benefits at the expense of the other.

Life experience teaches us that some people are "givers" and some are "takers". Givers are those who are generous with their time, attention, and resources, and try to help their fellow man.

Takers are quite the opposite. These folks rely on others for support, both physically and emotionally, and often economically as well. This is a spectrum of behavior and no one fits precisely into either category. However, most people belong more in one than the other, and empaths tend to be giving souls.

In life, high energy sources feed low energy ones. It is a law of the universe. Think about economics. People with a lot of wealth end up supplying those with little wealth through employment, taxes, and charity. They simply have more resources and buying power. Rich countries help support poor ones, and many citizens of financially distressed lands go to richer ones to earn money they send back home.

Think of families. The members with more energy contribute more to the family and those with less take more and give less. Many remember group projects in school where the hard-working student did the assignment for the whole group.

As an empath, it is vital that you understand that there are many kinds of takers, and some are much more treacherous than others. The most draining ones are a marked threat to any empath's wellness, and may be a major contributing factor to dysfunction. Identifying these "energy vampires" is an important step to mastering life as an empath.

There are five distinct types of Energy vampires (though some overlap may occur):

1. The Perpetual Victim/Blamer:

Lives with the belief that they are being controlled by external situations and people rather than being in charge of their own lives. This type consistently refuses to take responsibility for their actions and views themselves as persecuted and pushed around.

Often passive aggressive, they are extremely

negative, engage in self-pity, and like to rant about all the things that have happened to them. Sometimes they play the role of a martyr.

2. The Narcissist:

Describes people with an inflated sense of self-grandeur. They are greedy for attention and always seeking validation for their accomplishments. They become very angry when someone refuses to endorse their distorted perception of greatness, and may seek revenge.

This type rarely admits to wrongdoing, and will make excuses or blame others for their mistakes. Narcissists are extremely manipulative, can be charming and charismatic, and know how to get what they want. Some have insight into the fiction of their minds, but others genuinely struggle with understanding that they are not a superior life form.

3. The Jealous/Gossiper:

Focuses on tearing other people down because they feel bad about themselves. Instead of working on their own happiness, these people fixate on others' lives and spend their time talking about other people behind their backs, often in a critical manner.

They take a great deal of pleasure in gossiping, especially when other people are struggling. May pretend to be concerned about others' welfare and sad about their misfortunes, when in fact they are not sympathetic at all. They are notorious drama addicts, highly judgmental, and especially resentful of people who are successful and genuine.

4. The Dismal:

This Energy Vampire has an aura of doom and gloom. Being around these people instantly puts a damper on one's mood. This person is chronically pessimistic, highly insecure, and very anxious. They obsess about bad things that have happened, are happening now, and ruminate about the horrors inevitably waiting for them in their future.

They often have a compulsive need to verbalize their fears and are difficult to cheer up or redirect. The Dismal typically has poor motivation, low energy, and indulges in a sense of helplessness. They frequently find people to take care of them.

5. The Psychopath:

This is the rarest type and by far the most dangerous. These people are essentially predators and may be violent, abusive, or controlling. Hard criminals and con-artists fall into this category, and the more controlled ones may occupy high level positions. Their conscience is poorly developed, and they operate out of self-gratification and the pleasure principle. Consequences are the only thing capable of halting their predatory actions. They are potentially very dangerous to society.

It is important to understand that not all energy vampires are created equal. Some are more pathological than others, and some are more likely and able to change. For example, The Dismal is the most harmless of the bunch, because these people are by far the least malicious.

The others are more invested in actively hurting people in order to cope with their own insecurities, and the antisocial qualities of The Narcissist and The Psychopath make them by far the most destructive and damaging. These two types may be highly intuitive as well, and are not uncommon in spiritual circles where they use their intuition for selfish reasons. Empaths should be aware of this as they seek out literature and professionals for help.

Life sure has its challenges, and everyone goes through difficult times. A person may begin as an energy vampire and change for the better. Someone who usually copes well and has a positive outlook on life may turn into an energy vampire during an especially trying time in their lives.

This could be permanent or temporary, depending on the person. It is best to be compassionate and understand these people are only reacting to their own suffering. Still, allowing these people to harm you is unacceptable. Avoidance and/or eliminating contact with these people may be necessary.

Energy vampires are drawn to people like you, because they instinctually know that you are compassionate, will meet their needs, and that you are a rich source of energy. To put it bluntly: These individuals are like parasites looking for a host. They sense when they have found someone who will support them.

As an empath, it is your responsibility to protect yourself from these situations. The only reason an energy vampire is capable of harm is because it has been permitted.

Feeling drained and overwhelmed are key signs of contact with an energy vampire. Feeling guilty for not meeting their needs, ashamed of yourself, being anxious to help, and afraid of their reaction if one chooses to walk away from the relationship are other indicators.

Dreading a future encounter is a decided red flag that you are spending your time around someone who is not benefitting your existence.

Chapter 6:

Ways to Deal With Energy Vampires

As a sensitive, you need to understand that protecting yourself from anything draining is about self-preservation and wellness. Cutting off people who bleeds one dry is an indication of self-love, not hatred towards the other party.

Persons with weak immune systems avoid anyone or anything that could make them ill. It is simply common sense, and no one would think badly of them for avoiding health-threatening situations. Rather, it would be understood and encouraged.

Empaths who have not yet learned how to protect themselves are basically in the same boat. Unfortunately, that leaves a lot to be avoided, and other people are less likely to be as understanding and accommodating as in the first scenario. Therefore, let us go through some effective ways you can deal with Energy vampires individuals yourself.

As rough as it may sound to a sensitive soul, if the draining person is unnecessary, simply eliminate contact completely. Very often people continue to interact with those who do nothing for their quality of life out of habit or a sense of obligation. Not talking to your complaining neighbor anymore may be one of the best decisions ever, or maybe a new hairdresser must be found to replace a vicious gossiper.

The goal here is not to run away from anyone who is taxing, but to start being smart about what is allowed into your life. It is your life, after all. So much of what is sanctioned is not in one's best interests, and cutting out the dead weight can do wonders for happiness.

If the person in question is more influential, say a close family member, friend, supervisor, or co-worker, it is completely ok to mildly distance yourself instead, or "gently avoid". This means limiting exposure to the energy vampire as you simultaneously learn other coping skills.

As these people are avoided, do so with the proper attitude. Seeing them as powerful enough to drive you away is a mistake, as well as becoming resentful towards their behavior. Life is full of healthy and unhealthy options, and the choice has been made to go towards health. Value judgments will only fuel negative emotion in the long run.

The next steps are more active in nature, and are all about boundaries. Energy vampires are notorious for encroaching upon personal boundaries, and — as mentioned — it's your job, as an empath, to reestablish them. This may mean saying "no", politely disagreeing with an opinion, or refusing to work more than compensated for. It is time to speak up! It may require breaking a pattern that has existed for years. Sometimes the change is easy and you may wonder why they lived that way for so long.

If the changes you made are not appreciated, you will need to brush off the protests. This part can be unpleasant, but it is important to make yourself the priority, and not to succumb to old ways. Many energy vampires lean on empaths for support and assistance.

The empath often feels guilty at the idea of abandoning this role, and may even be tempted to try to introduce the person to a new way of looking at life or a positive support group. Though this being successful is not impossible, it is — in most cases — highly unlikely.

The truth is that most energy vampires actually don't want to change and get better. They want to remain as they are, and attempts to change them will only create more frustration. It is best to refrain from actively pushing to help them, and only offer these solutions if the person is making visible efforts to better themselves.

As boundaries are being established and your voice is being heard, there are other, more subtle techniques helpful to your transformation.

Psychic shielding is the practice of creating a protective cocoon or bubble that both keeps your energy separate and stops negative, intrusive energy from entering. It also prevents overload from excess stimulation and improves the ability to filter out helpful and unhelpful information.

It can be as simple as visualizing a white orb of sheltering light for a couple minutes every morning. When you overwhelmed or invaded, it is time to remember the shielding rays. Remember, anything that manifests in the world begin as thought, so this activity is creating the desired outcome.

A more comprehensive exercise is, "Ground, Center, and Shield". This can be used around energy vampires or any other difficult and debilitating situations:

1. Begin by focusing on the base of your tailbone.

2. Send energy there mentally and imagine a

steady foundation. Some people like to use the imagery of tree roots or visualize a cord connecting their base to the center of the earth. Others imagine red light shining from the tailbone towards the ground.

3. Next is centering. This can refer to the core (belly) and/or the heart. Both are essential to balance and energetic protection. The abdomen is like a storehouse for vital energy and is where our power and willpower reside. An open navel chakra makes one focused, determined, and successful. In fact, many problems affecting other areas will disappear when the belly is strong.

   The heart is equally valuable, and also serves as a place of balance. When we love, we live compassionately and understand how valuable each one of us is, including ourselves. An open heart will make one naturally protect oneself in a way that does not harm others. It is also a safeguard against psychic hypersensitivity.

   Focusing on or massaging these areas may be sufficient, or more visual people may prefer to see yellow and green light radiating, respectively, from the belly and heart center, or any other imagery or words that help.

4. The process ends with engaging the shield. The orb of white light may be seen in the inner eye. Another exercise is imagining wearing the world's most beautiful necklace or shield. It is so gorgeous and radiant that the light it casts disperses any negativity.

The Indian yogi Paramahansa Yogananda wrote about his life and training in his memoir, "Autobiography of a Yogi". When he was still in his youth, he spent a great deal of time with his guru. One night, he slept over at his master's ashram.

The mosquitoes were terrible, and Yogananda felt miserable while being swarmed by them. He approached his teacher for help, and realized his master was untroubled by the bugs.

The apprentice understood that his teacher had cultivated such focus that he could either will the mosquitoes away or be undisturbed by their biting. In a nutshell, the guru had lost his fear of the pests, and they could no longer harm him. He instructed his troubled student to lose his "mosquito consciousness".

The most effective and complete way to get rid of energy vampires is by changing yourself on a deep level. Working on confidence and self-worth while learning to view destructive people from a compassionate place is very powerful. When true compassion triumphs, one is able to see even the most immoral people as sources of light and truth. Trying your best to develop compassion for those who have been hurtful is another difficult but highly fruitful exercise.

At the same time, your ability to understand their motives increases, as well as the ability to understand that they are simply reacting to their own self-hatred and negligence. Doing all of these things will make you near impervious to harm.

When you come to recognize your own power, nothing anyone else says can deter you from what you know to be true and important. The inner spark of divinity has been acknowledged, and the naysayers appear more like gnats than anything else.

A truth that can take some getting used to, is understanding that people attract life situations towards them by the nature of their thoughts. Everything that manifests is a mirror of your internal climate, including surrounding yourself with energy vampires. If you are feeling attacked and drained, you must also be attacking and draining, even if it is directed at yourself.

The energy vampire's negative traits must also reside somewhere inside you. It's the concept that what seems to be coming towards one is actually coming from within. Every little thing in life is a chance to learn, and these troublesome individuals can be incredibly valuable lessons.

Another way to look at it is knowing that the universe likes to witness growth, and provides opportunities to overcome weaknesses. Impatient people may find themselves sitting in traffic or spending hours in a waiting room until they learn how to wait without fussing.

Empaths typically have a poor sense of self-preservation, and are much too hard on themselves. Energy vampires provide the chance to learn how to protect and self-nurture.

If all of the coping strategies fail, it is time to

further reduce contact. This also applies to significant people in your life. Ceasing contact with them temporarily or permanently may be the best course of action.

Chapter 7:

Cleansing Negative Energies

Good hygiene is recognized as an excellent way to maintain health and prevent disease. The same principle that applies to hand washing holds true for subtle energetic cleansing as well. When the system is functioning well, energy is used efficiently, and there is neither a deficit nor excess. The vast majority of people are operating on a fraction of the energy available to the human system.

Proper focus and discipline is necessary in order to tap into — and efficiently use — these energy reserves. One of the steps in doing so is making sure you are not being bogged down with excess energy. This is something that tends to happen to empaths, and the accumulation sparks a myriad of issues. Anxiety, panic attacks, depression, lethargy, and other health problems are all possible if extra, negative energy is not cleansed from the system.

Thankfully, there are multiple ways to clear your aura. If you're feeling heavy, burdened, or if being bombarded by external sources has been a problem, it is a good idea to clear on a weekly or even daily basis. In time, it will be easier to know when clearing is necessary.

A simple method is through prayer or use of a mantra. Many faiths have specific prayers or figures to call upon for protection, and this is an excellent way to accomplish your goal.

If this is not familiar, you can create a simple prayer asking that negative energy be removed from the system. Sacred sounds or "mantras" are recited to invoke what is being called upon. A Sanskrit mantra for protection of the body from oncoming danger is: "Om Hreem Hreem Hreem Hreem Hreem Hum Fatt". Chant this whenever you sense danger is coming towards you.

Smudging is another wonderful tool that has been around for ages. This is the burning of specific dried plants or resins whose smoke cleanses and drives away negative energy. Sage is the most well-known, but there are many different smudges including cedar, sweetgrass, lavender, mugwort, juniper, pinon, copal, frankincense, and myrrh. They have different properties, and can be combined for specific purposes. For example, sage is very good at cleansing, while sweetgrass is known to welcome positive energies.

Burning them together can be especially good. Smudge is either tied into a bundle called a "smudge stick" or comes loose and is burned in a fireproof vessel. Smudging is simple. Just light the smudge, blow out the flame, and pass or fan

71

the smoke over the whole body. After the individual is smudged, smudge the room, home, or area as well — to remove any lurking, stagnant energy. This is another good practice to do regularly.

A bath with sea salt or sage clears the aura in a similar fashion. Sage baths have traditionally been used for sore and aching muscles, but are also beneficial for cleansing. To prepare a sage bath, do the following:

1. Take three ounces/100 grams of dried rubbing sage and put it in cheesecloth, a cotton pillowcase, or a knee-high stocking.

2. Tie off the end and place it into a bathtub full of hot water, like a tea bag. Let the bag of sage become wet, wring it out, and repeat a few times.

3. Remove the bag and soak in the waters for twenty minutes or more. The bag can be dried and reused up to three times.

Gemstones can act as an alternative, as they are also capable of cleansing negative energy.

Fluorite is especially beneficial for removing bad energy from the aura, while amethyst and quartz balance and protect it. Placing a piece of selenite in each corner of the home after smudging can also be beneficial, as this creates a protective forcefield.

Amulets like a cross, yantra, or medicine wheel can be worn to ward off negative vibrations. Other tools like the mezuzah and hamsa hand can be used in the home to help maintain a positive energetic level.

Arts like feng shui are specifically designed to create harmony in one's living space. Empaths often feel like their home is their sanctuary and fortress against the world, but this can still be flooded by negative input. Deliberate arrangement and balance of the home optimizes how energy flows, and creates a rejuvenating place of rest.

If the negativity is triggering anxiety attacks, there are several simple, holistic steps you can take to help reverse the condition. They will be beneficial not only for panic attacks, but for any of the other symptoms as well:

1. Get deep, long-lasting sleep.

   Too many people neglect their sleep, especially now that technology provides 24/7 entertainment. Keep your cell phone and any other unnecessary technology out of the bedroom. Making good quality sleep a priority will work wonders for agitation. Having a set bedtime helps establish a rhythm that tells the body it's time to rest.

   Avoiding overstimulation thirty minutes before hitting the sack is ideal and doing anything that helps one unwind, like reading, journaling, or meditating, sets the tone for a restful night. Scents like lavender promote relaxation and rest, as well as chamomile tea and natural sleep supplements like valerian root.

2. Eat well and exercise daily.

   There are many, many diets and exercise programs out there, so keep it simple. Eat more fresh, wholesome foods with plenty of fruits and vegetables, and reduce or eliminate processed foods. Daily exercise can be as basic as starting the day with a ten minute walk or stretching.

More vigorous daily activity works wonders for some, and mind-body exercises like yoga and tai chi are especially helpful for empaths. Their movements are designed to balance and harmonize the body's energy on a subtle level, while also strengthening the physical body.

3. Do breathing exercises.

The breath becomes quick and ragged when under stress. The quality of the breath is a direct gauge of one's emotions and state of mind. Take some time to observe your breath and see how often it is unsteady. Simple breathing exercises will quickly calm the mind, and help the body to relax and re-center.

The following practice focuses on making the inhales and exhales of the same duration: Choose a count (four or six is good to start) and count to that number on the inhale. Exhale to the same count. Do this for a few minutes, or until the anxiety passes.

4. Avoid caffeine and other stimulants.

Stimulants may help with focus in the

short term, but make anxiety skyrocket in the long term. This includes coffee, tea and, yes, even chocolate. Furthermore, stimulants are hard on the adrenal glands, the anatomy responsible for the fight-or-flight response and buffering stress. Good adrenal health is linked to a healthy root chakra. Try switching to decaf, herbal tea, or lemon water.

5. Mindfulness meditation.

> The mind spends most of its time dwelling in the past or fretting over the future. Being mindful, or present in the now, is a panacea for the meandering and a cure for discontent. Mindfulness meditation can be performed when sitting quietly with crossed legs or in a straight-backed chair.

It really is as simple as it sounds:

a) As you are sitting, focus on the current setting.

b) Become aware of the sound of your breath, any other noises in the room, any smells or visuals.

c) Feel the cushion or chair under your body.

d) Any thoughts that arise in your mind are to be acknowledged and allowed to pass.

Doing this for ten or twenty minutes daily is recommended. It can also be done during any daily activities with the goal of being mindful in all tasks. When washing the dishes, for example, be present in the action. Do it slowly and lovingly. Be aware of every second of the action.

Mindfulness improves focus and reduces anxiety. It also makes people proactive instead of reactive. If an empath is being hit by a wave of input, mindful meditation will make it easier to think on one's feet and do what needs to be done to solve the situation rather than panicking and making it worse.

If an anxiety attack hits, grounding is the first step to take. Empaths can potentially receive waves upon waves of anxiety, and anchoring the system protects against external input. If this is ineffective, try mentally saying, "No!" with intent.

It doesn't matter if you know where the waves

are coming from or not. Refusing to allow the exchange can stop it dead in its tracks. Bending over and letting blood rush to the head will help with the spacey sensation, and tugging on the earlobes pacifies the system.

If you are at home or trying to sleep, wrapping blankets tightly around the body like a cocoon soothes and calms. Using any of the previously mentioned tools are an option, and sometimes all that is necessary is making contact with a close or loved one.

If nothing is working, let the panic attack end naturally. Acknowledge that it is only anxiety and cannot cause any serious damage. Say that it will pass in five to fifteen minutes if one refuses to panic.

Do anything to make yourself more comfortable and then wait. Remember that prevention is the best cure, and experiment with ways to do away with the episodes.

Humans are a part of the natural world, but it is easy to forget this as we walk around in our concrete jungles. Experts warned the public at the turn of the century that big city-living is detrimental to health. Spending time in nature is one of the simplest and most effective ways to rebalance the system, ground, and rid the body of stagnant energy.

It is especially important if you are currently residing in an urban area. Doing this regularly is a wonderful boost to health and happiness, and a potent preventative against falling ill.

Make spending time outdoors a regular part of your routine, and use this time as a source of pleasure. Bringing plants into your home and planting a garden are alternative or additional routes to take. Performing the aforementioned exercises in the wilderness can amplify their impact.

A more delicate matter is the healing of old emotional wounds. While the gifts of the empath are not pathological, many of the accompanying attitudes are. Poor boundaries, codependence, and being overly sensitive are signs of self-neglect. The empath who uses every technique available will only receive fleeting relief if old, underlying issues are not addressed.

They will be different depending on the person, and being brave enough to face these problems will be freeing in the long term. This kind of healing takes time and work, and may require a variety of interventions.

Alternative medicine, energy healing, and bodywork will realign your physical energies and assist with removing that which hurts. Psychotherapy is another option, and others find release in solitude, contemplation, and self-reflection.

The power of love should never be underestimated, and tender relationships can be highly transformational in nature. Devotion and surrender to the bigger picture can instantly heal pain that no other efforts have been able to touch.

Chapter 8:

Maintaining & Further Developing Your Gift

Intentional change always begins with awareness. The empath's world can be boggling, and life becomes much less so when the conditions are understood. Children sometimes become upset when unable to describe what is happening on the inside. Once they have words to convey their agitation, however, they quickly calm down, because what was once vague is now real.

Empaths live in a world they often can't describe. They doubt its validity, as well as their perceptions. Sensitives benefit greatly from observation, and understanding why they have been feeling what they have been feeling. Once that is established, the chaos is no longer chaos, but something with structure and patterns. Now there is something with rules, and this can be understood and mastered.

Learning about how subtle energy works gives you the theoretical knowledge to interact on multiple levels, without losing balance. Energetic tools and techniques give you practical skills to maneuver the environment effectively, and manipulate the subtle world the same way anyone would influence the material plane.

Acceptance is central. Without it, little progress can be made. This means accepting yourself and the whole situation. Reversing the self-neglect and choosing to see yourself as worthy can take some time. Fear of being egotistical often gets in the way of self-love, but it's the ego that makes one question one's own worthiness. The difference between self-loathing and a healthy regard for oneself is night and day. It is the difference between feeling tortured and being at peace. Choose peace.

What being a sensitive means for an empath in years to come can often provoke anxiety and fear. This can be a miserable experience, where the mind dreams up a variety of potential worrisome situations that are rarely based in reality. Relax. It's a journey. Start at the beginning and let the rest unfold.

Attend to what needs to be addressed now, and learn to be ok with uncertainty. Life is unpredictable already, so why does having empathic traits make this any different? People often run from themselves, but where is there to run to? It's like a hamster on a wheel.

A note of warning: People who ignore their gifts do not tend to fare well. Doing so is trying to escape a connection to something greater than yourself, and every individual always knows — on some level — that this is what they are choosing. It amounts to no more than burying one's head in the sand. Empaths who repress or ignore their experiences remain imbalanced, and are never truly happy.

Our wise friend from Chapter 2, the mythological scholar Joseph Campbell, loves to talk about something he called "The Hero's Journey". Campbell claimed that myths from around the world relating a sort of hero's quest always have the same fundamental steps.

It begins with the hero living a normal life, and leaving home when he feels urged to do. This nudge from the universe is "The Call to Adventure".

The hero then abandons the known world upon the answer of The Call, to undertake a mission in the uncharted territory of unknown and unexplored realms. On the journey, the hero faces tests, meets helpers, and — if successful — undergoes a personal transformation in which there is a newfound awareness and appreciation of the richness within.

The journey usually ends with the hero — now remarkably wiser from the ordeal — returning home, often to share their discoveries with humanity. This metaphor applies to any human who makes the bold decision to blaze their own path through the wilderness, in the attempt to find themselves and what life is really about.

Most people never receive The Call (at least in this lifetime), and for those who do, there is a choice to make whether or not to embark on it in the first place. The thing is, there's no journey (and no prize) if the hero refuses to answer The Call to Adventure. This potential hero has chosen the safe path, and will live the rest of their life with the sense that they missed out on their destiny.

Being an empath can be likened to receiving The Call. The choice of exploring a dimension to life that goes beyond the physical world is completely in your hands.

If you choose to embrace your abilities, being proactive is incredibly important. So much of the suffering empaths endure is due to reacting to circumstances. The situation "hits them", throws them off balance, and the empath strains to make the discomfort go away. It's a vicious cycle.

You may be so discouraged and exhausted that you struggle to find the strength to try to solve the problem. You may have become miserably content with managing symptoms, opposed to getting to the root of the problem. This is only putting on a band-aid, and becoming proactive will put the empathy back in control. You will benefit greatly from looking at your life and identifying the dynamics of difficult as well as positive situations.

Taking special precautions and working with multiple techniques may be necessary to successfully navigate the fields of energy. When you know of a difficult situation or person is in the near future, it is important to take whatever steps you need to neutralize the situation, or even turn it into a positive exchange.

Creating balance is the most complete way to thrive. This is embracing yourself as a whole being and operating on a physical, emotional, and spiritual level. People are multidimensional, and optimal functioning is experiencing wellness in all areas of life.

Health is good, work is satisfying, relationships are positive, finances are stable, and a connection to divinity is strong. One feels content and purposeful. Balance is relative to the individual and situation, and what balances one will not always work for another.

Take some time to evaluate current circumstances and decide what is balanced and what requires attention. If you are interested in using something more scientific, plenty of avenues are waiting. Experimenting with an assortment of techniques is not a bad thing, but trying to reinvent the wheel is usually a mistake.

There are already a multitude of systems that teach how to balance the system. Whether it is Traditional Chinese Medicine, Ayurveda, philosophies behind martial arts, naturopathy, contemplative prayer, shamanism, crystal healing, reflexology, reiki, or mindfulness doesn't really matter. All of these modalities come with theory, guidelines, tools, and a progression of steps to balance the body.

The experimentation involves figuring out which paths bring results. Be careful about trying to utilize too many different schools of thought, however. Many techniques complement one another, but each path utilizes different theories that drives the philosophy as a whole.

For example, tai chi teaches a completely different posture than yoga. Both methods work, and both techniques can be used, but it is impossible to follow one completely without contradicting the teachings of another. Another

Zen parable describes trying to master two different disciplines as a hunter who chases two rabbits, and catches neither.

Many empaths naturally gravitate towards the helping professions or volunteering, and this can be a perfect way to use your heightened empathy and compassion in a constructive way. Once a sensitive finds a balancing point, the empathy loses its capacity for self-destruction. Instead, it is like sharing one's light with the world.

Sensitive souls may be particularly suited to specific situations like working with the homeless, drug addicts, refugees, the terminally ill, or those displaced by natural disasters. Providing physical aid, comfort, and emotional support are wonderful ways to heal others and yourself. Animals may be more suited to certain empath's preferences, and environmental preservation could be perfect for another.

Empaths may provide spiritual guidance or direct their psychic sensitivities into such activities as astrology or intuitive readings. Engaging in important work is not always so obvious. The gift of sensitivity can be directed towards fellow human beings in any situation or calling. Working at a bank or gas station and treating every customer as a light-filled being is equally valuable. Consciously raising a family and teaching kin the value of empathy can be most suitable. The key is finding a situation that matches your talents and interests. Feeling content is a sign that this has been achieved.

Loving-kindness meditations, also known as "Metta", come from the Buddhist tradition, and are designed to develop compassion. Cultivating a sense of love and reverence for all in the universe — with no desire to have this returned — is the goal. Loving-kindness is first directed at the self, because loving others is near impossible without self-love. The practices will help you further develop your gifts, as they continue to open your heart and prevent burnout.

Here is an example of how to do Loving-kindness meditation:

1. Find a comfortable seat and take a few minutes to relax and become still.

2. Focus on the heart center.

3. Say, either mentally or out loud, "I am filled with loving-kindness". Picture yourself with a heart overflowing with

love and generosity.

4. Continue to repeat your affirmation and
    hold this imagery. Use any other words or
    visualizations that help support the sense
    of compassion. This should last fifteen to
    twenty minutes.

Practice regularly for a few weeks until you begin
to feel its effects. Once a sense of loving-kindness
for the self is established, move on to directing
this energy towards others. The first five or ten
minutes of the meditation remain directed at the
self, but the rest will then be spent focusing on
someone who summons forth feelings of love.

After practicing this for a few weeks, switch the
focus from a loved one to someone neutral,
possibly a stranger. This is a little more difficult.
The most challenging step is sending loving-
kindness towards someone who sparks feelings
of hatred and animosity. With time, attitudes
towards those who have brought harm into one's
life will soften, and eventually be replaced with
compassion and forgiveness.

Remember: What happens to one happens to all.
So, the greatest gift anyone can offer the world is
their own wellness. The universe simultaneously

carries individual and collective vibrations. A person's frequency is on a spectrum of positive and negative energy, and an individual's experience fluctuates as life circumstances change.

The strength of most people's light is medium, with some people casting weaker rays and other people casting stronger. This means that those with stronger vibrations are affecting the whole more significantly than those with feebler ones. The vibration can be anywhere on the spectrum of positivity and negativity, so someone with a strong vibration may be spreading good or bad energy.

There are a handful of souls in the world, most unknown, who shine forth such pure radiance that it counteracts most of the world's negativity, and prevents mankind from plunging into darkness.

Likewise, there exists incredibly malicious people who are harmful, and spread their hatred through mankind as a whole. With this concept in mind, flourishing as an empath is much weightier than one's own comfort.

Whether or not you choose to publicly use your

precious gifts is a personal decision, but — with proper balancing — honing your empathic traits and tendencies can only bring about good. Being compassionate in daily life is like infecting the world with joy. What may seem meager is not meager, not at all. Like a single lit candle, the smallest acts of kindness can vanquish the dark.

Conclusion

To sum up:

Being an "empath" is having a heightened sense of empathy, or the ability to identify with others' feelings and experiences. They often report feeling other people's experiences as if they were their own. Living and nonliving beings are made of energetic vibrations and have a field of energy that extends beyond the physical parameters. The fields of energy overlap and share the same space.

Empaths can feel the energetic interactions among different beings. They also have a sharper awareness that the universe is in fact a single mass of energy that manifests in many forms. In normal life, this oneness is experienced in terms of duality which the Taoists call "Yin and Yang", and the Hindus call "Shiva and Shakti". The two elements correlate with gender and the traditionally female strength of intuition is often viewed as inferior to masculine logic in many lands.

Being an empath has its advantages and disadvantages, but is ultimately a positive experience when balance is achieved. Avoiding common pitfalls like poor boundaries, giving too much, and being "too nice, too often" will bring greater happiness and steadiness to your life. Learning to ground and use the voice will stabilize your system.

Some people routinely drain the energy of others for themselves, and the most harmful ones can be described as, "energy vampires". Knowing how to protect yourself from these types of individuals is very important, lest you be burdened with ongoing anxiety and exhaustion.

Empaths tend to absorb nearby energy, and learning to energetically cleanse yourself improves overall functioning and wellness. There are plenty of options for clearing, like smudging, prayer, gemstones, or visualization. Once balanced, you have the option to develop your empathic traits, and finally use them for the betterment of yourself as well as others.

While this book is full of information and helpful exercises, none of them will provide lasting relief if you do not fundamentally change your worldview. Absorbing the agony of the universe is ultimately a choice, and all suffering empaths must carry a deep-seated belief that this is what they are meant to be doing. Otherwise, it could never happen!

It is fair to say that empaths either consciously or subconsciously engage in this behavior, because they think this is all they are good for and they deserve a painful existence. Being a sponge for suffering stops the second you truly value yourself enough to turn away the punishment.

The cleansing, shielding, and grounding methods previously mentioned will definitely help, but they can also turn into a crutch, and become a vicious cycle of absorbing and cleaning, absorbing and visualizing, absorbing and anchoring.

It is like trying to bail water out of sinking ship; it will keep you afloat for the time being, but the ship is still going down. Definitely use them as you work on your stamina and grow out of the addiction to tragedy, but never depend upon them as a cure. Developing your willpower and opening the rich energy in the belly is necessary for a long-term solution. Ideally, at one point, you will no longer describe yourself using this term. Instead, your empathic gifts will be recognized as a piece to a much larger puzzle.

Learning to tune into the positive vibrations of the universe is a practice. If one is completely absorbed in a book, it is possible not to be aware that the phone rang. The book was the only thing that existed and the phone was unheard.

Being alive is a similar process, in which the mind is trained to focus only on benevolent harmonies and automatically disregard the nonsense. When successful, the world and everyday, mundane life has a magical glow, where every little detail of creation is magnificent.

Identifying yourself as an empath is just the tip of the iceberg. There is a whole world at your fingertips waiting to be explored. It is good to remember that all people, sensitive or not, are the same at the core of being. Everyone possesses the same inherent worth, and is home to the same potentialities. If one could see the identical nature of the soul, people would cease to treat anyone else with contempt.

As an empath, you are more connected to the possibilities underlying the human condition, and this is quite exciting (if not a little intimidating). But playing it safe never pays off. The internal landscape is the most exquisite, and by far the most rewarding journey that can possibly be undertaken. Keep in mind that growth and change are processes.

This book hopefully served as a good introduction, but don't stop here. There are other resources out there with more examples, explanations, tips, tools, and techniques to help you with your search. Authors who write on the topic include Judith Orloff, Dr. Michael R. Smith, Elaine N. Aron, and Rose Rosetree.

The internet is full of blogs by empaths, and there exists various forums full of first hand empathic encounters. Reading biographies of famous empaths who mastered their gifts, like Edgar Cayce, can also be eye-opening. However, there is no book in the world that is a substitute for personal experience. Hiding in theory, books, or behind other people's experiences will not be fruitful.

After all, life is all about active engagement in one way or another. Get out there and participate! You'll be glad you did.

39944578R00059

Made in the USA
Middletown, DE
30 January 2017